BUNCH OF DAISIES

Daisy Neal

To: Rene.
with all good wishes.
From: Daisy.
15th October. 1998.

ARTHUR H. STOCKWELL LTD.
Elms Court Ilfracombe Devon
Established 1898

First published in Great Britain, 1997

British Library Cataloguing-in-Publication Data.
A catalogue record for this book is available from the British Library.

By the same author:
Poems of Praise and Promise
Pearls Within
Sing and Soar
A Ring of Rubies
A Bunch of Daisies

This book is dedicated to:—
My dear friend, Mrs Amy Buxton,
to celebrate her 107th birthday,
on 1st June, 1997.

ISBN 0 7223 3095-2

Printed in Great Britain by
Arthur H. Stockwell Ltd.
Elms Court Ilfracombe
Devon

CONTENTS

MY SPECIAL FRIEND

I have a very special friend, Amy is her name;
And few there are who too can claim,
Such a special friend as mine.
But some who read this little rhyme questioning will say,
The poet is too confident.
For why should I not have a friend,
Of whom I speak to all I meet, with joy and pride?
Because, dear reader, few there be privileged
To reach an age so great as my friend, Amy.
For when sweet flowers bloom on the first of June
And the larks sing high in azure-blue sky,
In this year of grace, nineteen-ninety-seven,
She will reach the age of one hundred and seven.

Daisy Neal

TIME WELL SPENT

Having written all the stories in this book, of incidents in my life which I could recall, I typed them out to send to the Publishers, but before packing them, I carefully read through each one in case there were any errors.

Coming to the one entitled, "No time to spare", I thought that it is too broad a criticism, for there are some people who do make time to show kindness to those who are old and lonely. And, indeed, this book has been written because of one who, although he must be very occupied in many ways, all day and every day, makes time every day to spare a few moments to give a little pleasure to someone unable to get out and about, who can neither see nor hear very well. He is the gentleman who runs the Home where dear Amy lives, to whom I have dedicated this book.

Some time ago he rang me and asked me if I had any more books like the two I have previously written for, he said, "Every day I read one of the stories to Amy and she loves them." I told him I did not have another book, but would try and write one. And so I set about it. But it takes a long time to write these stories, for I have to recall incidents which will make a good story.

However, I have now enough to make a little book, and I give thanks to the Lord Who has brought to my mind incidents, which I am sure I would not have recalled again, but for the need of them to make a story.

And so I would thank Amy's friend for his kindness to her which has resulted in this book being printed, and I hope they will both have much pleasure in reading the stories, and I hope they will be a blessing to them and to all who read them.

GOD'S PERFECT TIMING

When I was a very little girl, probably about four years of age, my mother was taken very ill with what was then termed, 'double pneumonia' and the doctor gave very little hope of her recovering, and came in two or three times a day to visit her. So Mother's sister had come to look after her and my father, my young sister and myself.

One day, the front door bell rang, and when Auntie opened the door, there stood a gipsy, ready to try and make a sale of some of the goods she was carrying, but, looking at Auntie's face, she said, "You look very troubled, Ma'am?" Now my auntie was not the type who would freely talk to anyone, let alone a gipsy, but this time was different, for her heart was full of anxiety, and she poured out her sorrow to this unknown gipsy woman, who, when she had listened to the story, said, "Ma'am, get some goose oil and give her a dessertspoonful with some orange juice with it, and rub some of the oil on her chest."

My father obtained some goose oil, from where, I do not know, but I suppose he went to a farm and got it, as farmers usually kept such medicinal things then. And so Mother took some, and more was rubbed onto her chest, and when the doctor called again, he just could hardly believe the difference in Mother's condition, and she gradually recovered — and lived to be ninety-two!

I have no doubt as to Who sent the gipsy to the door that day, at such a crucial time, have you?

Oh! He knows. He loves. He cares. Let us cast all our care upon Him, for He careth for us. Praise His Name!

THE PIG WHO BEGGED

When I was a little girl, many people kept a pig, although they had only a small back garden. Usually the gardens were long and narrow, as the houses were built in rows, and the pigsty would be at the bottom of the garden.

One day Dad told me he was going to take me to see a special pig which was owned by a man with whom he worked. So off we went after tea, one summer evening, and arriving at the home of Dad's friend, we were taken down the garden, which was, as I have described long and narrow, and the pigsty was at the bottom on the right-hand side, near to the back gate. Sure enough there was the pig, looking just like any other of his kind, and as we gazed at him he looked at us with his little beady eyes, and grunted, as much as to say, "Why are you all looking at me?" While I carefully scrutinised the animal, never having seen one at close quarters before, my father and his friend discussed the advantages or otherwise, of keeping pigs.

Then his owner took a piece of cake from his pocket and held it up above the pig's snout, and immediately the animal sat up and begged just as a dog does. Dad and I were intrigued. I can see it now as I write. A pig who begged. Who would have believed it!

But when I consider this I realise that, although he could sit up and beg, he was still a pig, the act did not change his nature one little bit.

There are many people like that pig, for they think that by doing certain things — charitable works, giving to good causes and such things, they are making themselves fit for Heaven. But they are mistaken, for our nature can only be changed by accepting the Salvation offered to us by the Lord Jesus Christ, by His death for us, when His blood was shed as He hung on the tree at Calvary. When we can say, "He died for me", then our sins are forgiven, the Holy Spirit comes to abide in our hearts, and we receive a new nature, "Old things are passed away, all things become new."

Yes, that pig I saw sat up and begged, but a pig he remained until he was killed, and hung up as sides of bacon on the rafters of his owner's kitchen. But we, who are sinners by nature are changed to be children of God when we accept the Lord Jesus Christ as our Saviour. Then we can sing the hymn sung at all Billy Graham's campaigns –

> "Blessed assurance, Jesus is mine.
> Oh! what a foretaste of glory divine.
> Heir of salvation, purchase of God,
> Born of His Spirit, washed in His blood."

EMPIRE DAY

In my childhood, the 24th May was celebrated as Empire Day, so called because of all the countries which came under the British flag, such as New Zealand, Canada and many other countries. Being then a very important day so far as Great Britain was concerned, all school children were given the day as a holiday.

In Stafford, beside the day being a holiday, a pageant was held in the Borough Hall, in which children from all schools in the town took part. Looking through an old diary recently, I had written for 24th May 1925, "We all celebrated Empire Day. I was dressed as an English lady." We performed little sketches, wearing the type of dress worn by people who lived in different countries in the Empire.

We also sang a lot on Empire Day, and one song I particularly recall was "Land of Hope and Glory, Mother of the free. How shall we extol thee. Who are born of thee." This particular one was sung by a choir of children who were chosen from all the different schools, because they were good singers. We went to St Mary's Church School to practise and the headmaster was the conductor. One line we could not get right as one word was off-beat: "Land of Hope and Glory, Mother of the free", and instead of 'Mother' being on two notes, it had to be sung quickly on one note. Could we get it right? We could not, and at last, in desperation the conductor hurled his baton across the room; but we got it right in the end.

There are those who criticize our nation about our colonies, but I know differently, seeing all the blessings received by the people who became part of the British Empire. Today there is strife amongst the people of almost every nation in the world, but one day, perhaps not far hence, an angel will proclaim, "The kingdoms of this world are become the kingdoms of our Lord, and of His Christ; and He shall reign for ever and ever." *Revelation 11 v15.* What a day that will be! A day when we read in *Psalm 86 v9.* "All nations whom Thou has made shall come and worship before Thee, O Lord: and shall glorify Thy Name." Then there will be 'Peace on earth, and goodwill to all men'.

"And the streets of the city shall be full of boys and girls playing in the streets thereof" *Zechariah 8 v5*

SKIPPING IN CORPORATION STREET

Any young person who reads the title of this story will undoubtedly, absolutely discredit the idea of children playing in a street, for they only know streets busy with cars and other vehicles, driving up and down. Recently, I went to Leamington where I had not been for some time, and I was appalled to see cars parked all along the edges of pavements, and a continual stream of them passing along the streets. Play in the streets!! Ridiculous! But that is just what children did in my young days. I will tell you about it.

When I first went to school there were three ways we could walk to it. The shortest way was over 'The Bank'. The Bank being a hill leading through allotments. Then there was the 'Middle Walk', a pathway between the several acres of allotments; it was quite wide but was muddy in damp weather. The last way was the longest way, 'Corporation Street', which was a mile in length. On one side of it were houses, and on the other side very high iron railings which enclosed an asylum with extensive grounds, with trees all round; really very lovely.

The Bank being the shortest way to school, we usually went that way, but in fine weather in spring and summertime, we liked to come home in the afternoon along Corporation Street, for there was no particular need for us to hurry home and we could play as we dawdled homewards.

Sometimes we played hopscotch on the pavement, but best of all we liked to skip in the middle of the road. This we did by having a rope from one side of the road to the other. One girl stood on the edge of the pavement on the side where the houses were, and another on the edge by the railings, each holding an end of the skipping rope, and while they turned the rope, another girl would skip in the middle. But at times the happy skipping was interrupted when a cry went up, "Pull the rope in, here's the baker." So one end of the rope was dropped and pulled across the road, and the baker, with his bread van, drawn by a horse, would pass by; then the rope would be thrown back and the skipping began again, but perhaps not for long, for another cry would go up, "Pull the rope in, here's the coalman." And he would pass by with his coal waggon stacked with sacks of coal. Then perhaps the milkman would come along with his special little cart, drawn by a horse, as were the others, and in his cart, churns filled with milk, for in those days, milk was delivered to our homes, and when the milkman came, we took a jug to the door and the milkman measured the milk into a pint can, and then poured it into our milk jug. Children of today have no idea of the way we older people lived.

And so we made our way home, skipping and stopping when the various horse-drawn vehicles came along. It was fun, and we were not only enjoying ourselves, but having healthy exercise. Moreover, we were safe, for our parents had no reason to worry about us if we were a little later home than usual, but we always arrived home at a reasonable time — certainly in time for tea, and with good appetites. What a lot the child of today misses!

But the time is coming when little children shall play in the streets of cities, and that will be when "The kingdoms of this world are become the kingdoms of our Lord and of His Christ; and He shall reign for ever and ever." *Revelation 11 v15.*

What a wonderful time that will be.

HOW TO MEMORISE

When my sisters and I went to school down 'The Bank', there was a stretch of road to walk along before we reached it. On the one side of the road was farmland, and on the other side two streets ran downhill from it, with houses on either side. From one of these houses a boy often appeared and he filled us with fear for he was always up to pranks. Now I realise he was just full of impishness, and liked to think he could frighten us, but really he meant no harm.

One thing he used to do I can never forget. When his mother sent him on an errand, he would skip all the way to the little shop which was on the corner of the street next to where his home was, and as he went he chanted, "Don't forget the candles, don't forget the lard, don't forget the butter," and this little chant was on the same six notes for each "Don't forget." I wonder if he sang the chant to the shopkeeper? I should not be surprised if he did.

I am wondering if it would not be a good idea if we made portions of Scripture into little chants which we could sing as we do our work. For example "Has not Jesus said, 'I will never leave thee nor will I forsake thee'." But I think the old hymns with their lovely tunes are better, and I am sure you will agree.

A few years later this lad, would no doubt, have had to go into the Army. I wonder if he chanted all the instructions given to him by the Sergeant Major? I should love to know what happened to that lad; such a one for teasing, and so lively but never really unkind to anyone.

THE SHEPHERD'S VOICE

My parents' home was near farmland, and as children my sisters, brother and myself loved to play in the fields, and in the springtime it was delightful, as there was a pathway which went right through the fields and up a hill called The Beacon, which was covered with bluebells. How we loved to pick some to take home to Mother. Are there any flowers which smell more sweetly than bluebells? Today, people are not allowed to pick them, are they?

Sometimes there were cows in the first fields where we played, and my brother, having listened to the farmer call them up at milking time, one day decided he would do the same, so he called, "Coop, coop" imitating the farmer. The cows stopped grazing and lifted their heads to listen, so he called again "Coop, coop," and this time they came walking slowly towards him, and we girls and other children fled and scrambled over the fence to safety. But Bob called again, and this time the cows came very warily towards him, then stopped, realising they had been deceived, looked rather accusingly at him and went on with their grazing.

As I recall this incident, I am reminded of *John 10 v4,5* where we read, "When He putteth forth His own sheep, He goeth before them, and the sheep follow Him, for they know His voice. And a stranger will they not follow, but will flee from him, for they know not the voice of strangers."

How careful we should be to listen to the voice of the Lord only from Scripture and avoid those who like to put their own interpretation to it. If we hold fast to Scripture we shall never go astray.

LOST – ALMOST

Always a nervous little girl, I had a strange fear that I might get lost. Why I do not know, and in any case it would have been very difficult for one to be easily lost in our town in my childhood, for it was then quite small, and, I would add, a lovely town in which to be born and bred.

Once, however, I was almost lost, but I was then a grown-up married woman, but oh! I was frightened, and I know you will laugh as you read about it.

It happened during the war when my husband and I were staying with our friend John and his wife. John had a smallholding, and near to his house a field of an acre; and as the Government had made a request for the growing of sunflowers, for some reason which I cannot recall, John had sowed this field with sunflower seeds. We went there towards the end of August when the seeds had grown into gigantic sunflowers, I had never seen such a sight before, and never expect to see a repeat of such a marvellous display. I should say the flowers were twelve feet high, or perhaps even higher.

We went with John to look more closely at this wonderful display, and while the men were talking, I thought I would like to walk amongst these massive flowers; so I walked in between them. No sky could be seen, just the huge heads of the flowers. It was a sight I shall never forget, and I am glad I saw it. I suppose John had scattered the seed in the first place, and they are not so large really, and the result was a whole acre of field just filled with these plants with the huge bright yellow heads.

After I had taken a good look around, filled with admiration and wonder, I decided to join the men again. I turned round, and then panic struck me, "But which way do I go?" This was something I had not considered as I looked round, and I now felt completely lost. Of course, I could have called out, and John would have heard me, but that idea never entered my head. Then, to my joy, I heard voices, and slowly I made my way in the direction from which they came. What joy to see my husband and John again. But it was very silly really, wasn't it?

Sometimes life brings difficult situations when we do not know which way to turn, but we have the assurance that if we lay the matter before the Lord in prayer, He will show us what to do. *Psalm 48 v14* says, "For this God is our God for ever and ever: He will be our guide even unto death." So do not panic or fear for the Lord will lead us in the right paths. Praise His Name!

THE OLD BUS

When we lived in Essex, we used to go sometimes to a little village where a few people used an old bus as their place of worship, and from time to time my husband was invited there to preach, and I loved to go with him. For one reason, it was a most unusual setting in which to hold services. But what most impressed me was the enthusiastic singing of these dear people. They were people who had little of this world's goods, but they loved the Lord and sang to Him with heart and voice.

The seating was long seats on each side of the vehicle, and, just as I have written this, I am wondering whether it was more likely to be a tramcar than a bus. Perhaps some of you who read this story will remember better than I do, how the seating was arranged in tramcars.

There is one chorus they sang which I well remember. It went thus —

"On Sunday I am happy,
On Monday full of joy,
On Tuesday I have perfect peace
The Devil can't destroy.
On Wednesday and on Thursday
I'm walking in the light,
On Friday it's a Heaven below
And the same on a Saturday night."

One time when we were there, an old lady sat next to me, and as we sang she thumped one foot on the floor and then the other in the rhythm of the chorus, as though marching, and the old bus shook.

How grand it is to be so joyful. The old lady certainly put all she had into displaying her joy in the Lord.

It gives us something to think about, doesn't it?

CASTING ALL YOUR CARE UPON HIM,
FOR HE CARETH FOR YOU 1 Peter 5 v7

Casting a net cannot be easy work, it takes much effort and strength and skill, and it was Peter, the fisherman who wrote, "Casting all your care upon Him, for He careth for you." Have you ever done just what Peter tells us to do? I have.

My sister was in hospital and I did want to go and see her, but not having a car myself, did not know how to get to the hospital, and I did not like to ask anyone to take me. The problem was much on my mind when I went to bed, and I lay thinking about it, and praying about it when suddenly Peter's words came to me, "Casting all your care upon Him for He careth for you." Immediately I got out of bed and stood up and said, "Lord, Peter said, 'Cast all your care upon You', and you know how I want to go and see Joan; so I am casting this matter on Thee," and as though I had something in my hand, I threw with all my strength, got back into bed and went to sleep.

In the afternoon there was a ring at my door, and who should it be but the minister of the church I attend. He said, "Joan is in hospital." Here I must point out that she lives in Leamington and attends the Baptist Church there, while I live in Warwick and attend the church here. And so, "Joan is in hospital," he said. "Yes," I replied. "Have you been to see her?" I said I had not. "Do you want to go?" he said, and I told him I did want to see her. "I'll take you," he said. "When would you like to go, tomorrow?" I agreed, and so we went.

I did not know, but there is no visiting on Thursday afternoons, but a minister can visit at any time. As we went in, a nurse said something to him, and she must have asked who I was for he said, "Her sister." We found Joan alone in the Day Room, and she was so pleased to see us, and we were able to spend a quiet hour together.

How wonderful! All this was arranged for me by my Heavenly Father and I do praise Him. Since that experience, He has arranged, what would seem to me to be much more complicated affairs, and I wonder at His goodness to me, and I prove, without doubt that "He cares for me".

CANNOCK CHASE

Cannock Chase is but a short distance from Stafford, and many happy hours have we spent there when we were children. On bank holidays, such as Easter, Whitsuntide and August bank holiday Monday, my parents hired a taxi to take us to Milford; only a few rich people owned a car in those days. There were five of us, myself, three sisters and our brother, the youngest.

For our little outing, Mother prepared piles of sandwiches, and from a little cottage by the Milford Common, we were able to buy a jug of hot water or a pot of tea.

On the Common which lies below the hills, there was always a fair with swings, 'dobbie' horses, coconut shies, in fact everything that is part of a usual fair, and parked here and there the gipsy caravans that brought all these entertainments. How beautiful those caravans were. All horse drawn, as motorised vans had not arrived in those days. Mother made friends with a gipsy lady named Mrs Smith, and she showed us the inside of her caravan, and it was splendid. All the furniture made from most beautiful wood which was polished and shone like mirrors. Oh! it was lovely. Mrs Smith was a big woman, very cheerful, and beautifully dressed so that she fitted in perfectly with her lovely home.

These gipsies worked hard. There was all the arranging and fixing up of all the equipment they brought with them, 'dobbie' horses, and swings, well, I am sure you will know what to look for at a fair. Then when the visit was over, all these things had to be dismantled, repacked and loaded to go to their next village or town.

As I think of these gipsy folk, my mind turns to Gipsy Smith, the great Evangelist. It was when he visited Bedford with his father when in his middle teens, he decided to come to Christ. He stood at the foot of the statue of John Bunyan and made this decision. He decided he would live for God and meet his mother in Heaven. But he wanted to make an open confession of his commitment to Christ, and this he did in Cambridge when attending a service in a small primitive Methodist chapel. During the singing of a hymn, Rodney, that was his name, went forward and knelt at the communion rail; as he did so, he heard someone say, "Oh, it's only a gipsy boy." What a dreadful thing for anyone to say. Little did they know that the gipsy boy kneeling at the rail would preach the Gospel all over the world, and thousands would be converted through his preaching. But an elderly man came to counsel him, and he said, "You know what you are doing? It is a great step to take, giving one's life to Jesus?" Well, Rodney replied, "I cannot trust myself, for I am nothing. I cannot trust in what I have, for I have nothing; I cannot trust in what I know, for I know nothing. It won't be hard for me to trust Jesus."

Rodney was sixteen when he took the Lord as his Saviour, and he could neither read nor write, but now he decided things must change and he bought three large books; a Bible, and English dictionary and a Bible dictionary. His family were amused. "Never you mind," he said. "One day, I'll be able to read them" and added, "and I am going to preach too."

And I heard him preach at the great Methodist gathering at Cliff College which always takes place at Whitsunside. It would be about 1935. What a thrill to hear him. He had a beautiful speaking voice and he spoke like a gentleman. He also had a lovely singing voice, and he sang, "How sweet the name of Jesus sounds".

Gipsy Smith is a perfect example of what the Lord can do with the most unlikely persons who yield themselves wholly to Him. Have you done this?

PICKING BILBERRIES ON CANNOCK CHASE

Cannock Chase I think, could best be described as being like a little portion of Scotland, and an incident which took place in this beautiful area, always comes back vividly to me when I think of it, and it concerns the mother of Vernon, of whom I have written in another article.

My husband and I were spending a few days with Vernon's parents when on leave from the Gold Coast, and it was late August, when the bilberries were ripe on the Chase. Mrs G suggested that my husband and I might like to go with her to pick bilberries. We were delighted to accompany her; and so she made some sandwiches and a flask of coffee, and we set off; the hills being only a short distance from the cottage.

Those who have picked bilberries will know that they grow on the ground amongst the heather, so it is necessary to get down on hands and knees for the job; so after awhile, a break for a drink and sandwich was very welcome. As we sat enjoying the refreshment, Mrs G told us a little about her life as a child. Her father was a farm labourer and worked hard, and so did her mother as they had a large family, and then came the Boer War. Some of the village lads joined the Army, thinking, I suppose, that there would be much more adventure in the Army than working long hours on a farm with little pay. Among those who joined up was a young man with whom Mrs G was very much in love, and he with her. But in those days, it seems, people had very little respect for soldiers, and Mrs G was forbidden to have any contact with him, and she was brokenhearted about this. Then, with tears streaming down her face she said, "One day, I knew that he had been killed," and this was later confirmed.

In those days, when couples had large families, they liked to get their daughters married in order to have more room in the small farm cottages, and so Mrs G's parents forced her into a loveless marriage. She told us all this, weeping bitterly. She was now a woman of around seventy, and yet all that happened those years ago was to her as though only yesterday.

We resumed our picking; she clambered above us up the hill, and we heard her singing, in a quavering voice;

"My faith looks up to Thee,
Thou Lamb of Calvary,
Saviour Divine."

This was her favourite hymn.

I conclude by this story that there are thousands and thousands of heroes and heroines whom the world will never know. But the Lord knows, and to such as Mrs G, He will say, before the host of Heaven, "Well done, good and faithful servant."

Vernon was a dear fellow, probably about thirty years of age when I first met him, but he was a mongol, and therefore treated by his family as though he had no intelligence, which was the usual way of treating such unfortunate people when I was young. His father was a farm labourer. They lived in a farm cottage; his parents and a sister a little older than Vernon. His mother was a charming, intelligent woman, and so was his sister. He had an older brother who was a Congregational minister, another was manager of a garage.

When my husband and I became engaged, he introduced me to this family, whom he had met at church, and as he was in lodgings he was often invited to their home, where he greatly enjoyed the family atmosphere, and I was welcomed with him.

Being there one weekday evening, I found Vernon's sister was making a rug, and I offered to help her, and she was pleased to have help; so every time we visited, out came the rug and I worked at it. One evening I was about to cut some wool, when I saw Vernon watching intently, and I paused and said, "Vernon, you could do this, couldn't you?" He nodded his head and grunted in his usual way, so I showed him how to wind it onto the stick provided for the job, and then how to slice it down the middle with the sharp tool to cut it. He got on fine, so, no more cutting pieces for me. Another time, I saw him watching keenly as I put the wool into the canvas, and I said, "Vernon, you could make a rug like this, couldn't you?" Another nod and grunt, and Vernon was now in the rug-making business, and many a rug he made for friends at church and others who heard of his skill as a rug maker. His life of idle sitting and doing nothing was over. Why had no one thought to see if there was anything he could do earlier. Of course, he did work on the farm during the daytime, but think of all the hours when he just sat, idle.

Sometimes after church, we would gather round the fire and sing hymns, and I would ask Vernon what he would like to sing; his choice was always the same, but only those who knew him could tell what he said. I wonder if you would ever guess? "Onward Christian Soldiers!" And how he loved to sing it in his way.

What friends Vernon and I became. Praise the Lord! I am always thankful the Lord used me in such an unexpected way, to bring such joy to a man who for so many years had lived such a dull, uninteresting life through lack of understanding. And I am so thankful that those so afflicted in these days are treated so differently.

BEFORE THEY CALL, I WILL ANSWER Isaiah 65 v24

Sometimes I find my Heavenly Father shows His care for me when I have not cast my care upon Him, in fact I have hardly had the opportunity to do so.

Just over a year ago, I had my kitchen completely refitted; everything was new, including the sink and taps. One Friday afternoon, the hot-water tap came apart, and in trying to hold the bottom half while screwing in the top part, I hurt the thumb of my left hand and had to remove a splinter of chrome which got down my thumbnail, it was bleeding and very sore. Just then the butcher's boy came to deliver my meat, and seeing my plight, asked me if I had any tools. I had, so handed him what he needed. He made a good job and I was grateful to him, but when he had gone, I realised it would not last long. Nearly 5-30 on a Friday evening. No plumber would want to be bothered at such a time.

Next morning, my Home Help came — with her husband! She had come that morning to put things back into cupboards now all the work in the kitchen was finished. I showed John my predicament. He asked for the bill I had had for the sink and taps, in order to get the name of the suppliers. I gave it to him. He then removed the tap and went off with it to the firm, which was a few miles from Warwick, and came back with a new tap which he fitted.

I said, "John, why did you come with Elizabeth this morning?" He said, "Because Elizabeth has been bothering me about things which need doing?" But I knew that he came because the Lord, Who knew all my need, had sent him.

"How good is the God we adore,
Our faithful, unchangeable Friend.
Whose love is as great as His power,
And knows neither measure, nor end."

CHRISTMAS EVE

I live in a first-floor flat, and it is a very lovely one. My sitting room has a big bay window at the front, and in it I have a cage on a stand, which is the home of my beautiful canary, Fryn. He is bright orange, with tiny black feathers round his eyes, which give them the appearance of having been pencilled round with mascara. Not only is he beautiful, but so is his singing.

I love Christmas Eve, for it is one of the happiest times for me, particularly if the sun shines in the afternoon, which it usually does, for I have a big side window through which it shines fully at this time of the year.

Over the mirror above my mantelpiece, and across to little pictures at either side, I hang a string of fairy lights, which are little chariots of all colours, and how beautiful they are when lit up, each having the tiniest little bulb inside.

Picture me then, settling into my chair by the side window, sun shining on me, chariots glowing, my little radio beside me, waiting for 3 p.m. What am I waiting for? The Nine Lessons and Carols from King's College, Cambridge. How I love these carols and the Scriptures read so beautifully from the Authorised Scriptures. And what does Fryn do? You can guess. Sings and sings, overcome with joy. He loves every minute of it, and so do I.

"Sing choirs of angels,
Sing in exultation.
Sing all ye citizens of Heaven above.
Glory to God in the highest.
Oh! come let us adore Him,
Oh! come let us adore Him,
Oh! come let us adore Him,
Christ, the Lord."

I am sure little Fryn adores Him with all his voice, and I do with all my heart, as I do not sing, for if I did, I should not hear Fryn, and I would not like to miss his exuberant joy.

COUNTRY FOLK

I love to think about the dear friends we had when we attended a very small Methodist chapel, situated in a very rural setting. It had been built in the days when Nonconformists were not welcomed by the Established Church, and there was opposition to them buying land in villages for building a church. Because of this, farmers often gave a piece of their land on which a church could be built, and some of them were in rather strange positions.

The one I am writing about was built on a corner of a field known as Mrs K's seven-acre field, and as a lane ran alongside the bottom of it, it was a very convenient spot for access to the chapel. The lady's husband had died, and she continued to work the farm herself with the help of a man, and she ploughed this huge field herself.

She was a very tall woman, and big too, and she played the little organ for the chapel services. How the stool held her as she pedalled away with great vigour, I do not know, but I never heard that it collapsed — furniture was made to last in those days! When we were on leave from the Gold Coast, on our first visit to this dear little chapel, Mrs K said, "You never oughter-a-went!" So we knew how she summed up the situation.

The farmer and his wife had three little boys, and one Sunday we had been to tea with them, and were walking along a little path through a field, when the youngest boy ran ahead, climbed up a little tree which was growing at the side of the pathway and called out, "Mummy, say, Zaccheus, come down." There was no Sunday School at the chapel, as these were the only children, but they knew the Bible stories well, and always came to the services with their parents.

Another time, being on leave and visiting our dear friends, walking across a field, Mr W said, "Mr Neal, I remember in 1936 you preached on" — and named the subject. We were astonished that he should remember after so many years, what had been the subject of my husband's ministry at that particular time. But there were no tractors for ploughing in those days, it was all done with horses who pulled the ploughing machine and as the farmer steered them down the furrows, he went over in his mind the sermons he had heard the previous day. No wonder there were so many fine Christians amongst the farming people who attended the little Methodist chapels.

Let us praise the Lord for John Wesley, the Founder of Methodism.

SAVED BY A PARROT

When my husband and I left the Gold Coast, one of the scientists from the Research Institute where my husband worked, was in Nigeria working there for a time, so we were unable to say goodbye to him and his wife, before coming home.

The time came round for them to take their annual leave in Scotland, where they lived, and they boarded a plane at Lagos Airport. The plane took off, rose up over the mountain, and whether it came suddenly upon unexpected cloud is not known, but it crashed and all passengers and crew were killed.

At home in England, we heard the news of the tragedy, and then we saw a report in a newspaper. There was a picture of a man with a parrot perched on his hand, and the caption was, 'Saved by a parrot'.

The story related concerning the picture was, that the man was booked to come home on the plane on which our friends were travelling, but the captain refused him permission to bring the parrot with him, so the man stayed behind as he would not be parted from the bird.

What a dramatic story! I have often thought of that man, and whether he saw the Lord's hand in this marvellous way his life was spared, and thanked the Lord for His goodness to him. Parrots often live to a good old age. I wonder how long that bird lived?

As you read this story, can you look back and recall times when the Lord has intervened in incidents in your life, and if not saved you from death, from making decisions or mistakes not beneficial to you? I am sure you can. Then praise Him and give Him all the glory. He is worthy.

"COME YE THANKFUL PEOPLE, COME"

I am sure there are experiences in the lives of all of us which always clearly remain in our memories. Such times for my husband and I were the Harvest Festival Services held in the little Methodist chapels in the country villages. Some of the chapels were very small; in one we attended regularly, apart from Harvest times, it would only hold about twenty-five people. Regular worshippers there were, a farmer, his wife and two sons. The organist, whose husband had died and she did the farming; the village policeman and a gamekeeper, and three or four more people, and my husband and I went whenever we were free, as my husband was often preaching in other churches and I always went with him. In larger villages, however the churches were bigger. But in our young days, there was one thing the same about all the village chapels – they were lit with oil lamps, and had a big, round black coke-burning stove for heating. But how beautiful these chapels looked when decorated for Harvest. I will try and give you some idea of how they looked.

Below the pulpit, on each side of it, there was a sheaf of corn, and then all along the bottom of it, flowers of autumn; chrysanthemums, Michaelmas daisies and other late flowers. Then there was a table in front with bowls of eggs, plums, apples and all other country fruits. Along all the window ledges there were similar bowls of fruit and vegetables and vases of flowers. Oh! the lovely fragrance which came from all these fruits of the earth! But I am writing about country chapels, and there was another odour which mingled with the flowers and vegetables. Can you guess what it was? The smell of the oil lamps! If you have never breathed in the blending of these two aromas you will never be able to imagine it. Unique, and never to be forgotten!

One incident at a Harvest Service I shall never forget. The preacher asked the children present, what they liked best of all the things they saw, and one little lad called out, "Spud Tarters," which brought laughter from all present. "Isn't there anything you would like better?" said the preacher. Doggedly the answer was returned, "Spud Tarters." There is nothing like having one's mind made up on a matter, is there?

People of today who only know a Harvest Service where tins of baked beans and peas and fruit are displayed, cannot possibly imagine a Harvest such as I have tried to describe to you, for at such times we were truly thankful for the Lord's bountiful gifts of the fruits of the earth.

But Harvest did not finish on Sunday evening in the village chapels, for on Monday was the Harvest Supper. What rabbit pies those farmers' wives could make! What would I not give to taste one now! And with the rabbit pies went wonderful fellowship. Oh! we were thankful in those days, and with our thanks, there was also much joy.

NO TIME TO SPARE

Have you noticed that in these days, in spite of all the aids to easy living — cars, washing machines, dishwashers and other items, few people have even a little time to give for a friendly chat with anyone they may meet, especially if the person is old and may chat a little too long, being pleased to exchange a few words with a friend. And when some of these dear old saints are no longer able to attend church, it is sometimes the case that only a routine visit at Christmas can be expected.

In my home town, there was a dear old gentleman who attended the Baptist Church. He had been the owner of a sweet shop and was generally known as 'Toffee Sharpe'. When he retired he spent nearly all his time visiting aged people. He was a great friend of my parents, and when I was on school holiday once, he suggested I might like to go visiting with him sometimes. I agreed, and how glad I am I went with him, for going into the 'Visiting Business' opened up a new life to me. How he had come to know all the people we called on, I do not know. I remember one old lady who lived at the end of a row of little cottages, reached by a very narrow little pathway running off a very busy main road.

And so I started to learn the art of visiting, with dear old 'Toffee Sharpe' as my kindly teacher — not that he said anything to me, I just took mental note of the way he went about his business. I recall how, after a while those on whom we called, when they saw me, would say joyfully, "Oh! you have brought the little girl." And then he suggested I might sing to them, and this became an added bonus to the visit, for how they loved to hear the old hymns which they loved so much.

I particularly remember a lady who lived in a little terraced house with just a pavement between the front door of the house and a busy main road; and just a few houses below the one we visited were the great entrance gates to Stafford Gaol. To visit our friend we went up two high steps straight from the pavement, to get to the door of the house, and the door led right into the room where she lay in bed.

This lady was not so old, perhaps about forty, but she had been in bed for many years with what was described as 'Chalk Rheumatism', and her face looked like chalk, but she did have a little colour in it. She was lovingly cared for by her mother, and the linen sheets were always a spotless white. I can picture her now as I write.

Her face always lit up when she saw 'Toffee Sharpe' and 'the little girl', and when the little girl sang a hymn, the mother leaned on the rails at the bottom of the bed and listened with great satisfaction. I indeed had excellent training in visiting the lonely and sick people, and I do so wish I could get about now to do it.

After I married I continued visiting, going around on my bicycle. One lady I went to every week spent her time in the small back bedroom of her niece's council house, but at least she had an interesting view of the gardens of neighbours' houses.

Sometimes I left my washing on the line when out visiting, and there were occasions when the rain fell while I was away; alas! So arriving home I had to gather in wet washing to dry indoors. But that was part of life before washing machines which dried clothes were invented. But there was still time to visit! Amazing, isn't it?

SAFE TRAVELLING

I do not know what is carried by rail today, for it would seem to be that the bulk of goods are carried by road in huge lorries, but in my young days a great variety of goods were moved around the country in what were called 'Goods trains', and as far as my experience goes some of the 'goods' were very unusual, but all arrived safely at their destination.

For instance there were children who often travelled long distances 'In care of the guard'. I did myself when going to stay with my uncle and auntie who lived just outside London, but came to London to meet me. Dad and Mum took me to Stafford Railway Station, found the guard of the train on which I was to travel, told him where I was going and who would meet me. He then took us along the train and looked in all the carriages to see what type of people were there already, chose one he thought suitable and being satisfied, saw me seated and then went off on his duties. But at regular intervals he came along to see if I was all right. Once I remember there was a little boy travelling on his own also, but we were too shy to speak to each other. At the end of the journey I was safely handed over to my relatives. Presumably the guard considered keeping his eye on little lone travellers as part of his everyday duties.

And then there was a strange, lone traveller which was sent to us from friends who lived in the country in Essex, and this was a pheasant. He was dead, still in his feathers with his legs tied together, and delivered to our home. It was a nice present, but I had the job of plucking him and preparing him for the table, and it was a new job to me, and as you will image, not a very easy one for a novice. I have forgotten whether we enjoyed it.

But I am sure you would never guess what was the most valuable package ever delivered to us from Stafford Station.

When my husband and I married, we wanted a canary, but it had to be a Roller; if possible a German Roller called a Gluck Roller, if I remember rightly; but being unable to get one in Stafford, we were given the name of the secretary of the Roller Canary Club who lived in London. We wrote to him, but he said it was really the end of the season for buying birds, but he had one which was a very free singer but not quite up to competition standard. He said he would send it to us, and if we were not satisfied we could return him. So the bird was sent to us, and how do you think he came? In a little box by rail. He was brought to our home from the railway station in a goods van, which delivered all goods sent by rail. The driver knocked our door, handed the little box to me and said, "I hope he is all right?"

We had a cage ready for him so I opened the door of the cage, then the flap of the little box, and without hesitation the bird hopped into the cage, right onto a perch, and what do you think was the first thing he did? He sang!!!! How wonderful! He did not hop round the cage and examine it, or look for something to eat and drink, he just sang.

Think of all the hours that little bird was enclosed in that small box with no room to turn round, all in the dark, and nothing to eat or drink. All the way from London he came; then the wait while the delivery van was loaded, and the driver may have delivered other goods before he came to me. All that before freedom came, and then to sing.

You will be interested to know that this little bird lived to the age of fourteen. Quite a good age for a canary. And he certainly fulfilled his reputation of being a 'free singer', but why he was not up to competition standard, we never found out.

I am sure we can all learn from this little bird, and resolve to take up the 'singing habit' whenever our Heavenly Father sees us through difficult situations, after times of sickness, indeed at all times let us sing;

"I feel like singing all the time,
My sins are washed away;
For Jesus is a Friend of mine.
I'll praise Him every day."